The Leeds and Liverpool canal has for some two hundred years stretched across North West England uniting many of the industrial towns of this region and though not conceived as a single engineering project it gradually developed into a lifeline some 127 miles long. With its many branches and connections to other navigation systems it brought considerable prosperity to this area.

The canal is still navigable and though not now commercially used, its future is no doubt secure as a recreational source.

Text and Photographs © by
David C. Lyons 1977

Published by
Hendon Publishing Company Limited
Hendon Mill, Nelson, Lancashire

Printed by
Fretwell and Brian Limited
Howden Hall, Silsden, Yorkshire

Liverpool's Collingwood Dock (left), reached by the canal after passing under the swing bridge (right) was not the intended terminus. It was opened as a branch line in 1846, necessitated by railway expansion during this period which threatened disruption to the original route to Old Hall St. and the Princes Dock area.

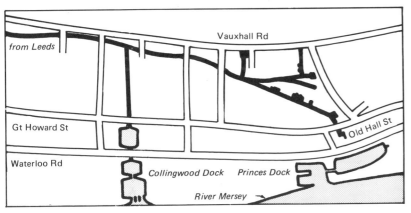

from Leeds

Vauxhall Rd

Gt Howard St

Old Hall St

Waterloo Rd

Collingwood Dock   Princes Dock

River Mersey

Because of the rebuilding of Exchange St. Station, considerable alterations were later made in 1882 to the Old Hall St. terminus. Originally the canal continued into a cluster of basins flanked by wharfs and warehouses but it is now truncated (left). The canal has since been filled in (bottom left) though the towpath, bridges and mooring rings still exist.

Railings and barbed wire as seen at Sandhills Bridge are commonplace in Liverpool. Access is virtually impossible.

In 1929, overhead power line gantries were built along the canal from Stanley Dock locks to Litherland and have become such a familiar part of the skyline in north Liverpool.

The new 'Triad' office block towers over the older buildings alongside the canal at Bootle. Swans are present here and show the first signs of wild life that become increasingly more common.

A procession of some twenty eight boats and barges pass through Aintree advertising the Inland Waterways Association.

The canal becomes more accessible at Maghull and young fishermen, ducks and modern houses are now seen at the water's edge.

Northwards between Ormskirk and Southport, the land is extremely flat.

Originally the plan was to cut a waterway along this plain from Liverpool to Preston and from Preston northwards up the Ribble Valley towards Clitheroe. It would have been a relatively easy task but the route did not allow the canal to serve the larger industrial areas around Wigan and subsequently new plans were considered.

Regrettably some craft lie abandoned on the canal bed; of no further use, except to show that the canal is not always as deep as it often appears.

The canal had a saucer shaped cross-section when constructed and although constant efforts are made to ensure it is kept navigable, a certain amount of silting up has inevitably occured.

(Right) the River Douglas, shown here, passes under the aqueduct carrying the canal near Parbold and Newburgh.

Possibly started as early as 1753, this section of the canal known as 'Leigh's Cut' was intended as a by-pass to the River Douglas, running nearby. The Douglas had been made navigable in the first half of the eighteenth century to take coal carrying vessels from Wigan to Preston but the canal was to be an improvement to this existing navigation. Eventually Leigh's Cut became part of the Leeds and Liverpool canal.

(Left) the terminus of the now disused Tunnel Branch at Wigan.

Work was in progress during May 1977 to measure an old set of lock gates. Wooden beams were placed above the lock to halt the majority of the water and sods of earth were then shovelled in further damming the flow. The locks then fully exposed were made accessible for repair.

The Leigh Branch shown in the centre of the picture (below) travels to Manchester and the canals of the south leaving the Leeds and Liverpool south of Wigan.

Bullrushes make an unexpected but very pleasant appearance along the banks at Wigan.

(Below) a barge passes through the Johnson's Hillock flight of locks which connects with the original Lancaster canal navigation, the north end of which terminates after only a short distance (left). Known as Walton Summit branch it is not now navigable. This section of the Lancaster— from here to just north of Wigan and passing to the east of Chorley—was taken over by the Leeds and Liverpool around the beginning of the nineteenth century, finalising this part of the route's construction which hitherto had caused considerable problems.

Feniscowles near Blackburn. (Above) the remains of an old swing bridge and (right) grooves in the masonry of a stone bridge showing where the tow ropes of horse drawn barges have worn over the years.

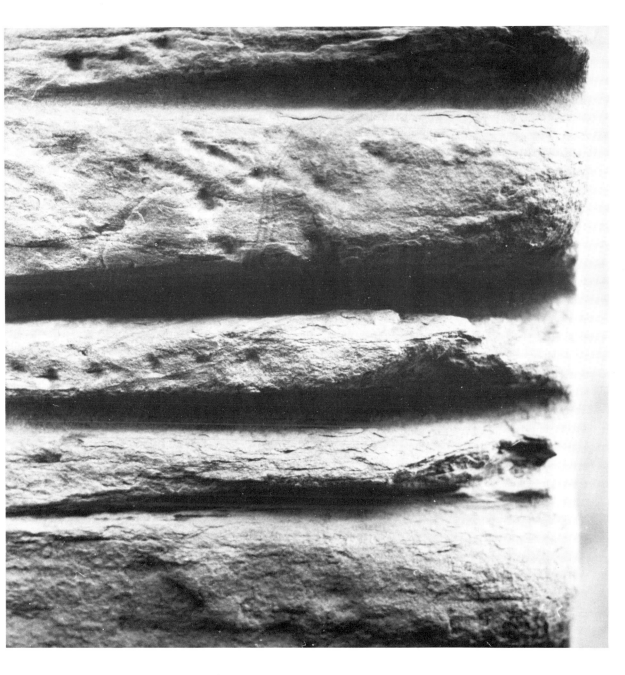

The canal passes through Blackburn, away from the new town centre but adjacent to this old building with its splendid towers. At ground level however the new metal locks have become subject to the now common defacements.

(Right) a canalside warehouse at Rishton.

Church (left) and Clayton-le Moors (centre and right) make an eerie sight when the buildings are photographed as reflections in the water.

Both pastoral and industrial scenes within sight of each other. Taken at sunset, the farm and power station reflect the glasslike stillness of the canal.

(Left) Slater Terrace in Burnley became the subject of consideration as a 'Lancashire' museum. The terraced houses opening directly onto the canal bank could certainly not provide a more fitting location.

The Watts clock tower overlooks the canal as it circumnavigates Burnley centre.

(Far left) Manchester Road bridge from an old wharf. (Left) the view as seen from Ormerod Road along the aqueduct at Burnley. The aqueduct's embankment rises some 46 feet above street level and the majority of the soil was acquired from the deep cutting and 559 yard long tunnel at Gannow on the opposite side of the town. Having crossed under the road (below), the canal takes in the scenery of Thompson's park around which it travels.

Although vast changes are taking place west of Brierfield as the new M65 is prepared, the canal is obviously well respected. But for some strengthening along its bank and the unfortunate loss of an old stone bridge replaced by a temporary flat span over which construction vehicles pass, it is left completely untouched.

St. Mary's Church, Carr Road Bridge and canal side buildings at Nelson.

Barrowford locks, where seven flights carry water down from the summit level (the highest section of the canal) to the long lock-free southern stretch. During the considerable dry spell in 1976 it was common to see views as this below. The summit level has occasionally in the past been closed through lack of water.

(Right) the Anchor Inn at Salterforth with the canal frozen over.

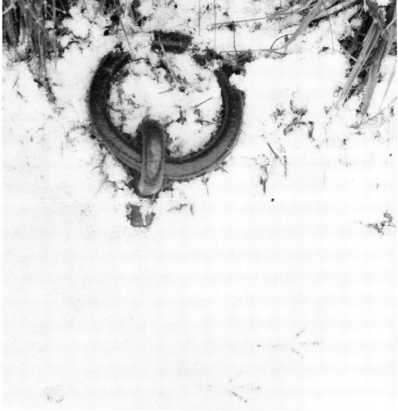

Lake Burwain and other reservoirs supply the necessary water to the summit level. (Far left) the lake during the dry summer of '76 was extremely low. Yachtsmen were somewhat frustrated though anglers were more than happy! Pendle Hill and Blacko Tower are constantly to be seen in this vicinity.

Foulridge Tunnel, between Barrowford locks and Salterforth was opened in 1796. It had taken five years to complete the 1,640 yards and is of course still extensively used by motorised pleasure craft. Initially it was necessary to 'leg' barges through whilst the horses were lead overland to the opposite end.

The front cover was not taken at night but is in fact a view looking directly into the tunnel.

Greenberfield, north of Barnoldswick has three locks which start the descent from the summit level eastwards towards Skipton and Leeds. Originally there was a three rise staircase similar to that at Bingley but this was replaced in 1820 to conserve water at this level.

(Right) a peculiar double arched bridge supporting the A59 under which the canal passes at East Marton.

Locks by the A65 west and east of Gargrave where hire boats out of Skipton first learn to manoeuvre through and cope with the correct proceedure of the lock gates.

(Right) an angling competition one Sunday morning shows one extent to which the canal is now being used.

Skipton—and four views along the Spring's Branch or Lord Thanet's canal—a branch constructed in the late eighteenth century so that materials from the quarry behind the castle could easily be transported to the main canal. (Far left) a disused chute protuding from the castle wall at the terminus.

The canal follows the line of trees along the hillside on the left having departed from Skipton and heads towards Keighley via Kildwick. This was one of the first navigable sections of the Leeds and Liverpool canal proper, being opened in 1773.

(Left) a swing bridge near Kildwick.

(Right) gardens leading to the lakeside and swans make this section at Keighley unusually pleasant.

A very famous landmark on the canal's route is the five rise locks at Bingley. Barges wishing to travel through must expect to take about half an hour to negotiate the flight although most pleasure craft hesitate at the task.

Locks allow the canal to slowly descend as it skirts Leeds centre until (right) finally the last lock, seen in the centre, opens into the much wider Aire/Calder Navigation.

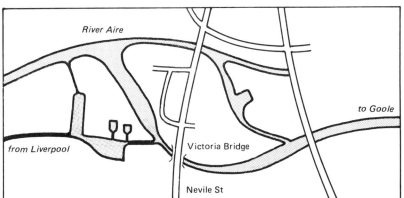

River Aire

to Goole

from Liverpool

Victoria Bridge

Nevile St

With the Aire/Calder Navigation and the estuary at Hull the canal helps to effectively disect England with a continuous waterway from west to east.

Industrial use of the canal may have declined but so much is presently happening along the entire length that its future seems safe for a long time.

LEEDS LOCK

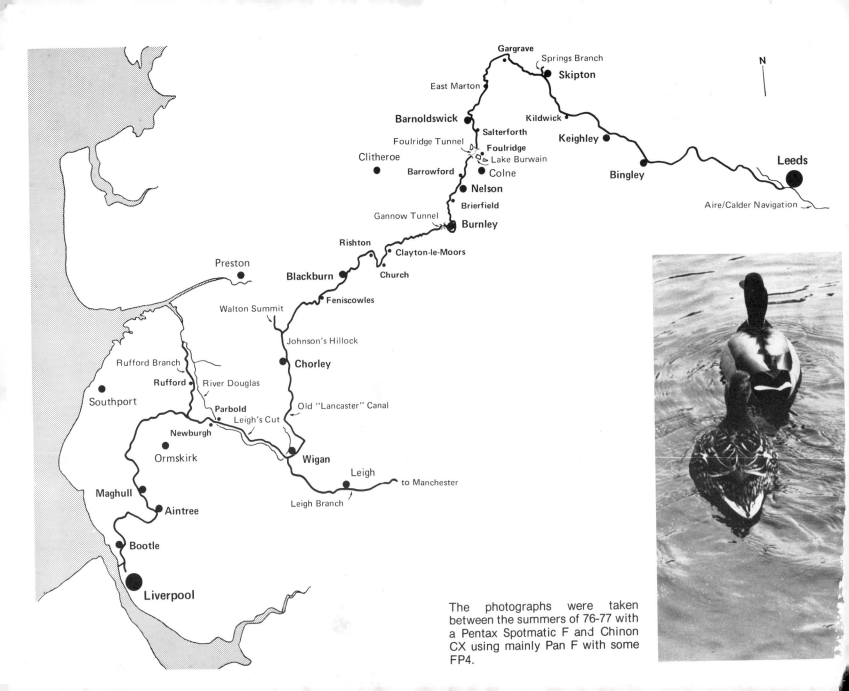

N

Gargrave
Springs Branch
Skipton
East Marton
Kildwick
Barnoldswick
Keighley
Salterforth
Foulridge Tunnel
Foulridge
Lake Burwain
Clitheroe
Colne
Bingley
Leeds
Barrowford
Nelson
Brierfield
Aire/Calder Navigation
Gannow Tunnel
Burnley
Rishton
Clayton-le-Moors
Preston
Church
Blackburn
Feniscowles
Walton Summit
Johnson's Hillock
Rufford Branch
Chorley
Rufford
River Douglas
Southport
Old "Lancaster" Canal
Parbold
Leigh's Cut
Newburgh
Ormskirk
Wigan
Leigh
Maghull
to Manchester
Aintree
Leigh Branch
Bootle
Liverpool

The photographs were taken between the summers of 76-77 with a Pentax Spotmatic F and Chinon CX using mainly Pan F with some FP4.